REPAIRING
THE WORLD

The **12 Days** of
Christmas with
FRANCIS &
CLARE of **ASSISI**

REPAIRING THE WORLD

The 12 Days of Christmas
with FRANCIS &
CLARE OF ASSISI

BRUCE G. EPPERLY

Anamchara Books
Vestal, New York 13850
www.AnamcharaBooks.com

Paperback ISBN: 978-1-62524-854-1
eBook ISBN: 978-1-62524-855-8

Illustrations by Bernardo Ramonfaur (Dreamstime.com).
Design & layout by Micaela Grace.

CONTENTS

1

FRANCIS AND THE FIRST CHRISTMAS CRECHE

As an author, I look back to moments of inspiration, when the idea for a book was born. Sometimes, it's an invitation from a publisher. Other times, it's an insight that comes out of the blue while I'm taking my predawn walk. Still other times, I chance upon a quote, story, or scripture that changes the way I look at a subject, inspires me to action, and alters my understanding of the world. In the case of this book, I came upon a story from the life of Saint Francis that I had read during my research on Francis, but never truly noticed, until the Christmas of 2021.

I had been looking for a theme around which to structure my personal reflections for the Twelve Days of Christmas, a spiritual practice I have followed for the last several years. I was in search of a spiritual focus that would enable me to immerse myself in the Christmas season long after the presents have been unwrapped and the tree taken down. I was astounded when I read that Francis may have created the first Christmas creche. Synchronously, in this account of Francis and the Christmas creche, I found my inspiration.

On a cold December day, as I was listening to Christmas carols after dropping my two grandchildren at the school bus stop, I came upon some words from Saint Bonaventure, one of Francis's most illustrious followers. Bonaventure's account changed the way I looked at Francis and his mission—and invited me to spend twelve days, plus the Feast of Epiphany, with Francis and his spiritual companion, Clare. I will quote them in the archaic language of the philosophical Bonaventure, who penned one of the first biographies of the saint from Assisi:

> Now three years before his death it befell that he
> was minded, at the town of Greccio, to celebrate
> the memory of the Birth of the Child Jesus, with
> all the added solemnity that he might, for the kin-

dling of devotion. That this might not seem an innovation, he sought and obtained license from the Supreme Pontiff, and then made ready a manger, and bade hay, together with an ox and an ass, be brought unto the spot. The Brethren were called together, the folk assembled, the wood echoed with their voices, and that august night was made radiant and solemn with many bright lights, and with tuneful and sonorous praises. The man of God, filled with tender love, stood before the manger, bathed in tears, and overflowing with joy. Solemn Masses were celebrated over the manger, Francis, the Levite of Christ, chanting the Holy Gospel. Then he preached unto the folk standing round of the Birth of the King in poverty, calling Him, when he wished to name Him, the Child of Bethlehem, by reason of his tender love for Him. A certain knight, valorous and true, Messer John of Greccio, who for the love of Christ had left the secular army, and was bound by closest friendship unto the man of God, declared that he beheld a little Child right fair to see sleeping in that manger. Who seemed to be awakened from sleep when the blessed Father Francis embraced Him in both arms. This vision of the devout knight is rendered worthy of belief, not alone through the holiness of him that beheld it, but is also confirmed by the truth that it set forth, and withal proven by the miracles that followed it. For the ensample of Francis, if meditated upon by the world, must needs stir up sluggish hearts unto the faith of Christ, and the hay that was kept back from the manger by the folk proved a marvelous remedy for sick beasts, and a prophylactic against divers other plagues, God magnifying by all means His servant, and making manifest by clear and miraculous portents the efficacy of his holy prayers.

According to scholars, prior to Francis creating the first Nativity scene in 1223, common people would go to mass on Christmas to hear the story of Jesus' birth recited in Latin, a language they neither spoke nor understood. Francis invited some of the crowd to wear costumes, as townsfolk and local sheep and oxen gathered around a wax figure of the infant Jesus. As Francis told the Christmas story in the language of common people, tears fell, and miraculous events occurred. Long before the Hallmark Channel's "Miracles of Christmas" movie series, the transforming spirit of the Child of Bethlehem, as Francis called the infant Jesus, transfigured hearts, minds, and hands, and brought joy to the world. Eyes opened, and relationships healed.

And so it is still, for those for whom the doors of perception are cleansed. The Infinite Love of God bathes all things with its radiant beauty as we see the Godhead incarnate in a newborn child.

The words of Howard Thurman, the subject of my first Twelve Days of Christmas meditations, describe the first Christmas and its impact on those who see beyond the glitz and glitter:

> There must be always remaining in the individual life some place for the singing of angels—some place for that which in itself is breathlessly beautiful and by an inherent prerogative, throwing all the rest of life into a new and creative relatedness—something that gathers up in itself all the freshets of experience from drab and commonplace areas of living and glows in one bright light of penetrating beauty and meaning—then passes. The commonplace is shot through with new glory—old burdens become lighter, deep and ancient wounds lose much of their old, old hurting.

A crown is placed over our heads that for the rest of our lives we are trying to grow tall enough to wear. Despite all the crassness of life, despite all the hardness of life, despite all the harsh discords of life, life is saved by the singing of angels.

Clare, like her older spiritual companion Francis, is a guide for seekers in our time. Francis was her lifelong friend, and with his help, she established a convent for women, where, at the age of twenty-one, she became the abbess. For the next forty-one years, her wisdom reached out to shape others, including popes and bishops—but she herself never left the convent. The Child of Bethlehem had lured her from privilege to simplicity and from physical beauty to the greater beauty of holiness. Francis's spiritual equal in an era when women were maligned as intellectual inferiors and occasions of sin, Clare's deep spirit and sharp intellect still inspire holistic spirituality, balancing Francis's spirituality of pilgrimage with a spirituality grounded in one place. Clare, like Francis, heard the singing of the angels.

Christmas is a matter of vision—seeing, hearing, tasting, smelling, and touching beyond appearances to discover that all things reveal the love of God. In the humblest manger or most advanced medical setting, whether on the U.S. borderlands, in an urban slum, a Cape Cod beach, or in a suburban Washington, DC, mansion, the Christ child is born.

A week after I read the story of Francis and the Christmas creche, I encountered randomly—or was it by Providence?—another story that captures the spirit of the Twelve Days of Christmas. On a cold January morning in 2007, an apparently undistinguished man played six Bach pieces on his violin as a couple thousand people passed through a DC Metro station, most on their way to work and oblivious to their surroundings. In the forty-five minutes he played, only a handful of people stopped; he collected a mere $32, tossed thoughtlessly, for the most part, into his violin case. Few noticed when the unidentified musician concluded his concert. The Metro Station continued its usual frenetic chatter, unaware that the anonymous violinist was Joshua Bell, one of the greatest musicians in the world, who had been playing some of the most intricate Bach pieces on a violin valued at 3.5 million dollars. This event was organized by the *Washington Post* as part of an experiment about perception, taste, and people's priorities. Beauty and wonder, a concert worthy of inspiring radical amazement not to mention an expensive ticket, filled the air, but only a few passersby noticed. The rest passed by, oblivious to the revelation in their midst.

Surely, this is what the Twelve Days of Christmas proclaim: Beauty and wonder are in this place, our world—but how often do we, like the commuters that day in the train station, overlook the coming of the Child who changes everything?

When we do notice, however, this ordinary baby transforms everything. A new light shines, and a star guides our paths. Our lives are illumined, and amazement fills our spirits. We want to be this Child's companions in bringing beauty and healing to our troubled planet. We want to follow him to Bethlehem, Galilee, Jerusalem, and into the streets, bistros, places of employment, and Halls of Congress, saying with Francis and Clare, "Peace be with you."

May you who read this book once again hear "the singing of the angels." May you be refreshed and renewed and ready to repair this world, taking your role as an artist who works alongside not only Francis and Clare but also the Poet of the Universe.

2

FRANCIS'S INCARNATIONAL SPIRITUALITY

Francis and Clare were unlikely saints. As young people, they had everything going for them. They were all that most people hope to be, then and now: talented, intelligent, well-liked, affluent, good-looking, and upwardly mobile.

They even dressed well! Yet God spoke to them, as God speaks to all of us, and they listened and discovered an unexpected path: the pathway of simplicity, spirituality, and service. They left the life of affluence to follow the Child in the manger.

Young Giovanni di Pietro di Bernardone of Assisi, Italy (1181–1226), was born into privilege. His father Pietro was a successful trader in cloth and fine fabrics, a member of the rising upper middle class. His mother Pica was, by all accounts, intelligent, compassionate, and lovely. Young Giovanni's parents had great hopes for their son: he would inherit and expand the family business and, like all good sons, support his parents in their old age. Although he was a bit of a wild child, Giovanni's parents anticipated that their son would eventually settle down, learn the virtues of frugality and profit-making, marry well, and enjoy a comfortable life. They expected that he would be respected in the community and ensure that their grandchildren would be achievers.

Giovanni, known as "the Frenchman" because of his wardrobe and interest in all things French, enjoyed the privileges of economic and social status. He inherited a life much like that of many upper-middle-class young people today: parties, good food, leisure to enjoy his friends' company, the latest toys and gadgets, sports, and the goal of rising beyond his current status through acts of courage and loyalty on behalf of the regional elite. Francis was known to be generous to friends and strangers alike, always saving a few coins to toss to beggars on the street after a long night of partying. Despite his generosity, no doubt Francis of Assisi, like many in our society today, took his privilege for granted as deserved and God-given. Only later did Francis let go of his social and economic privilege so that he could live in solidarity with all creation, rich and poor, human and nonhuman.

Although he was assured of financial success, Francis wanted more. He dreamed of fame—and in his day, the pathway to fame was found in knighthood and military success. Francis aligned himself with a local nobleman and went to war on his behalf, but he failed as a knight. His forces were defeated, and Francis was imprisoned. With time on his hands, Francis began to ponder his future. Would he return to the military, and continue his quest for wealth and power? Or would he find another path, one that focused on the holy adventure of self-discovery and companionship with God?

As Francis pondered his future, a voice called out to him, "Who can do more good, the master or the servant?" When he replied, "The master," the voice continued, "Then why are you looking for the servant rather than the master?" This was the beginning, for Francis, of a transformation that continued on throughout his entire lifetime.

Repairing the Church

Just a mile down the hill from the town of Assisi is the Chapel of San Damiano. Seeking Divine guidance, Francis sojourned to the dilapidated chapel to pray. Again, he heard the voice of God, once more coming as a question demanding his response: "Do you not see that my house is falling into ruin? Go, therefore, and repair the house out of love for me." Francis, still rooted in a practical, this-world outlook, took God's words literally and went to work physically rebuilding the Chapel of San Damiano and two nearby chapels.

Then Francis went a step further: while his father was away on business, he helped himself to some of the expensive cloth stored in his father's warehouse. He sold both the fabric and his horse, planning to use the gold to continue his work of rebuilding the little chapel. When Francis's father returned home and discovered what his son had done, he was furious.

Francis's father took his complaint to the bishop, who summoned Francis to appear before him. The bishop tried to reason with him, explaining that God would not want him to steal from his father to do God's work. "My son," said the bishop, "have confidence in the Lord and act courageously. God will be your help and will abundantly provide you with whatever is necessary."

These words so inspired Francis that he stripped off his clothes in front of the entire assembly and handed them to his father. Standing naked before the crowd that had gathered, Francis turned to his father and said, "Until now I have called you my father, but from now on I can say without reserve, 'Our Father who art in heaven.' God is the only wealth I need, and in God, I place my trust."

Having renounced his right to his father's wealth, Francis returned to gathering stones to rebuild the chapel. Over time, however, he discovered that God had a greater mission in mind: God intended for him to rebuild the spiritual church by returning Western Christianity to the simple gospel of Jesus of Nazareth.

Growing in Wisdom and Stature

Two moments from Francis's early spiritual adventures reflect his evolving spirituality. Like most healthy people of his time, Francis was repulsed by the skin disfigurement that leprosy caused. On one of his journeys, when he encountered a person with leprosy, he was initially revolted and worried he would be contaminated by the contact. But then something shifted inside him—and Francis dismounted and embraced the leper. Shortly thereafter, Francis traveled to a leper colony, where he begged forgiveness for his alienation from the residents there and left them with the kiss of peace. From then on, people with leprosy became a unique focus on his ministry. This movement from alienation to solidarity, so pivotal in Francis's spiritual transformation, challenges our own incivility and alienation from those who differ from us, whether in race, economics, health, or politics. In embracing the leper community, Francis discovered that there is no "other." Beneath the distressing disguises of others, he found Christ. We too, when we encounter people who are different from us—whether they are people without homes who are living on the street, immigrants, people we disagree with politically, or even leaders who seem unable to do their jobs well—will discover the face of Christ.

A second moment that reflects Francis's spiritual growth comes when he counsels his spiritual companions to travel by foot rather than horseback. In Francis's time, differences in status in military and civilian life were reflected in the contrast between the upper class, including religious leaders, who traveled on horseback, and commoners, who went by foot. Francis leveled the spiritual and social playing field: a follower of Christ, he believed, must be united with the poor and vulnerable, living as they do and seeing the world from the perspective of the marginalized and impoverished. As Francis embraced simplicity in attire and travel, he expressed his solidarity with all humanity, regardless of status or economics. What matters is the Spirit, the presence of God in all God's children, Francis realized, and not the external and superficial differences that get in the way of our relationships with our fellow humans, hiding our essential oneness in the body of Christ.

The Peaceful Prophet

Francis's ministry was countercultural. While he chose not to be an ecclesiastical activist who publicly challenged the institutional and clerical corruption of the Roman church, Francis's focus on simplicity of life and poverty presented an alternative to the values of the Roman church of his time. It called its leadership to transform its values and practices to reflect more fully the simple life of Jesus.

Francis also opposed the Roman church's support of the Crusades' violence. When Francis and his spiritual companions blessed anyone they encountered with "May the Lord give you peace" or "Peace be to this house," their words resounded far beyond individual relationships to the affairs of church and state. In a world of violence and never-ending wars, Francis sought to build a culture of peace. He worked to support the Realm of God with this-world justice based on healthy interconnections between humans and between humans and God.

Francis's first biographer, Thomas of Celano, described the mystic activist as "always new, always fresh, always beginning again." But saints seldom wish to be called saints, and mystics are hesitant to boast of their spiritual experiences. Aware of their fallibility and temptations, they seldom take adulation and publicity seriously. Accordingly, although Francis was venerated as a saint in his lifetime, he constantly directed attention away from himself to God. Francis knew his weakness and imperfection; he recognized the distance between God's call and his response. He also knew that accepting adulation and fame was itself a burden that could get in the way of our relationship with God. Francis often confessed his humanity and imperfection to highlight his solidarity with those who daily struggle with temptation and ethical failure.

Living the Gospel Way

But Francis did not set out to be an ecclesiastical or social reformer. Instead, like reformers and prophets throughout the ages, Francis experienced the living God—and with that encounter, he, like Isaiah, Jeremiah, Amos, Sojourner Truth, Martin Luther King, Desmond Tutu, and Dorothy Day, received God's vision of a new spirituality grounded in an alternative reality to society's injustice, inhospitality, and materialism. Seeking to live in accordance with the gospel lifestyle of Jesus and his first followers, Francis discovered the profound dissonance between the powerful and wealthy religious empire centered in Rome, the legacy of Constantine's marriage of church and state, and the simple hospitality and egalitarian ministry of Jesus of Nazareth.

Francis walked the talk. He advised his fellow monks to preach the gospel message with their actions, not just their words. Faith without works is lifeless, Francis knew, and admonition without action is useless; we must practice before we preach. Whether he was speaking to nobles, peasants, sparrows, or fish, Francis's message joined contemplation with action and teaching with transformation.

Today, Francis still challenges us to prophetic restlessness as we view the inequalities, injustice, and environmental destruction of our time. He shows us other alternatives to the way we live our lives.

Facing Death and Finding Peace

Facing physical decline and disability, Francis experienced Christ's stigmata, in which the wounds of Jesus transformed his own woundedness. Francis's physical suffering connected him with the suffering God, the fellow Sufferer and intimate Companion who understands our pains, the One who feels our every joy and sorrow and seeks our healing even when there cannot be a physical cure.

Francis believed that even death and the process of diminishment can be portals to Divinity. In his final days, Francis added a verse to his Canticle, describing "Sister Death" as praising God. Even in death's shadows, Francis recognized the gentle, friendly face of Jesus. Inspired by the Infinite and Eternal Reality in whom he lived and moved and had his being, Francis accepted his own death with joy. Knowing his times were in God's hands, how could he, like the nineteenth-century poet Robert Lowry, keep from singing?

> **What tho' my joys and comforts die?**
> **The Lord my Saviour liveth;**
> **What tho' the darkness gather round?**
> **Songs in the night he giveth.**
> **No storm can shake my inmost calm**
> **While to that refuge clinging;**
> **Since Christ is Lord of heaven and earth,**
> **How can I keep from singing?**
>
> **—Robert Lowry**

3

CLARE'S ILLUMINATING VISION

Like Francis, Clare of Assisi (1194–1253) was an unlikely saint. Born Chiara Offreduccio, Clare came from wealth and yet sought poverty. She became a respected spiritual guide despite the misogyny of her era, during which the spiritual elite viewed women as inferior vessels of God's grace. Although her relationship with Francis, her senior by twelve years, is shrouded in mystery, I believe Clare was Francis's spiritual sibling, or *anamcara,* whose feminine spirituality of rootedness complemented Francis's spirituality of pilgrimage. Canonized in 1255, she was described by Pope Alexander IV:

O Clare, endowed with so many titles of clarity! Clear even before your conversion, clearer in your manner of living, and exceedingly clear in your enclosed life, and brilliant in splendor after the course of your mortal life. In Clare, a clear mirror is given to the entire world.

Born to Italian aristocracy, Clare was the subject of a prenatal prophecy. Apprehensive about carrying her first child, her mother went on a pilgrimage to pray for a safe birth. While she was at prayer, her mother received a Divine message: "O Lady, do not be afraid, for you will joyfully bring forth a clear light to illumine the world." This prophesy led her family to name her Clare, or Chiara, meaning "clear" or "bright one." She grew into a lovely woman, the object of desire of many suitors, but despite her family's pressure, Clare refused to marry. She said she was saving herself for the wealthiest and most worthy Spouse, Jesus Christ. In doing this, she was not necessarily rejecting motherhood and wifehood so much as she was choosing a life path that would allow her to pursue her own interests.

When Clare first heard Francis speak, the itinerant preacher's vision of voluntary poverty as a pathway to encountering God and serving the world inspired the seventeen-year-old. At eighteen, to the dismay and anger of her family, Clare left home to follow the monastic path forged by Francis several years earlier. Like her spiritual sibling, Clare abandoned the world of wealth and social status to devote herself solely to the riches of divine simplicity.

Until her death in 1253, Clare spent virtually all of the rest of her life cloistered in the monastery of San Damiano, the first church Francis repaired. Clare gathered around her a community of women who were also committed to following Jesus through sacrificial living, voluntary poverty, and universal hospitality. Her commitment to women's spirituality and the affirmation of women as spiritual equals to their male counterparts makes Clare a forerunner of today's feminist theologians.

While Francis and his companions were pilgrims, traveling throughout Italy, seeking to reform the Roman church and spread the gospel, Clare and her Poor Sisters were cloistered, living in an enclosed community, committed to a life of obedience, poverty, and charity. Clare's spirituality of place reminds us that every place can be the holy of holies and every environment an invitation to Christ-like living. You don't have to leave home to experience spiritual transformation.

Transforming Relationships

The relationship between Clare and Francis has given rise to much speculation. On the hand, Clare looked up to Francis as a mentor and teacher, and described herself as Francis's little plant. On the other hand, Francis and Clare have been characterized as spiritual companions, integrating the feminine and masculine, as well as the introverted and extroverted, dimensions of spirituality in their relationship. Undoubtedly, as Clare matured, their relationship would have changed. While Clare still listened to Francis's wisdom, now Francis also sought Clare's spiritual guidance.

According to legend, Clare and Francis once met for a meal in Portiuncula, a chapel in Assisi. The local inhabitants were amazed when a blazing fire emerged from the place. When the townspeople sought the source, they discovered Francis, Clare, and their companions caught up in mystical ecstasy. Francis's and Clare's relationship testifies to the transformative power of spiritual friendships between men and women. Passion can inspire and shape our spirits, not just our bodies, elevating us to union with the Divine.

A Spirituality of Equality

Clare's cloistered life was both a choice and a necessity. Social convention dictated that Clare's movements were circumscribed in contrast to the peregrine spiritualities available to men. While the tradition of courtly love of Clare's time romanticized the relationship of women and their suitors, women were generally considered intellectual and spiritual inferiors, often described as "occasions of sin" who tempted "weak" male religious seekers from the pathway of celibacy. Women traveling alone or in groups were also at risk of attack and harassment. In describing the spiritual status of women in the twelfth century, Franciscan scholar Ilia Delio, in her biography of Clare, asserts that "women were seen as a source of sin as secondary images of God." Delio goes on to say that women's souls were judged as deficient, "defined through their bodies alone, they were not capable of being an image of God." Despite these spiritual and intellectual stereotypes that privileged the male mind, Clare had the audacity to speak of women as created fully in God's image, capable of attaining the same level of spiritual devotion as their male counterparts. According to Delio, Clare saw "herself as an image of God and capable of union with God because the word became

flesh and she herself was flesh." Clare affirmed herself—
and all women—as revelations of God's glory, glorifying
God through their very existence.

The Power of
Downward Mobility

Like her spiritual companion Francis, Clare championed
voluntary poverty. Born into financial and social privilege,
she saw the renunciation of wealth as a pathway to spiritual transformation. Clare realized that trusting God alone,
rather than possessions, awakens humans to God's intimate
and providential presence in their lives. She understood Jesus' counsel: "Where your treasure is, there your heart will
be also" (Luke 12:34).

During the most materialistic season of the year, when
Black Fridays and Tech Mondays figure far more promi-
nently than Jesus' humble birth, Clare reminds us to place
our ultimate trust in God and not in our material security—or the gifts under the tree.

Downward mobility strips away everything that stands
between us and God. The gift of simplicity gives birth to a
sense of God's nearness. Delighting in the beauty of the earth
and the joys of friendship, Francis and Clare embody a deep-

er materialism, the vision of the Incarnation, the Christmas vision of all things as holy and worthy of love and reverence.

Gazing on Jesus

Clare counseled the royal Agnes of Bohemia—and us still today—to "gaze" upon Christ and then from that gaze come to imitate him in the world by mirroring God's love in daily life. This "gazing" upon Christ, as both an infant and a grown man, leads to a merging of vision and action.

Clare counseled her companions to "place your mind before the mirror of eternity. Place your soul in the brilliance of glory." Clare invites us to go to the manger and gaze upon the loving mother, the protective father, and the vulnerable baby who is our Healer. Seeing then leads to acting. Clare sought to walk in the footsteps of the world-loving, outcast-embracing, healing-dispensing, crucified Christ. Christ's willingness to sacrifice power and perfection for our well-being inspired her sacrificial life.

Clare would have affirmed Paul's Christological hymn from Philippians, chapter 2, as representative of God's love for us and our calling as Jesus' companions. Clare lived out this hymn as she sought to let Christ's mind guide her every footstep.

Let the same mind be in you that was in Christ Jesus, who, though he was in the form of God, did not regard equality with God as something to be exploited, but emptied himself, taking the form of a slave, being born in human likeness. And being found in human form, he humbled himself and became obedient to the point of death—even death on a cross. Therefore God also highly exalted him and gave him the name that is above every name, so that at the name of Jesus every knee should bend, in heaven and on earth and under the earth, and every tongue should confess that Jesus Christ is Lord, to the glory of God the Father.

In embracing Christ's cradle and cross, our souls expand to embrace the whole earth. Wherever we are, we are in God's presence. We become Christ-like in our love for the world, and we experience heavenly splendor in the challenges of daily life, as well as the promise of eternity in every encounter. In simplicity of life, seeing God's presence in ourselves and in our marginalized kin, we become God's companions in saving ourselves and the world.

Five centuries after Clare, another spiritual foremother, Ann Lee, inspired the Shaker hymn, "Simple Gifts," penned by Elder Joseph Brackett (1797–1882). This hymn reflects Clare's spiritual vision and enables us, like Clare, to come 'round right.

> *'Tis a gift to be simple, 'tis a gift to be free,*
> *'Tis a gift to come down where I ought to be,*
> *And when I am in the place just right,*
> *I will be in the valley of love and delight.*
> *When true simplicity is gained,*
> *To bow and to bend I will not be ashamed.*
> *To turn, to turn will be my delight,*
> *'Til by turning, turning, I come 'round right.*

Clare invites us to spiritual inquiry as we celebrate Christ's birth. Her vision of spiritual decluttering challenges us to go beyond the glitz and glitter of the Christmas season to see deeply into the life of the baby Jesus, letting the Child of Bethlehem illumine our daily lives.

During the twelve days of Christmas, Clare and her spiritual companion Francis ask us to consider the following questions:

- Where do I see Christ in my life and the world?

- What activities bring me joy?

- What stands in the way of me experiencing joy?

- What clutters my life, spiritually?

- What clutters my life domestically, around my home?

- What one action can I take to simplify my spiritual life, enabling me to experience God more fully?

- How can I live more simply to protect the environment and promote the well-being of others?

Clare recognized that embodying the spirit of simplicity is a lifelong process. But she also knew that as we become more downwardly mobile, living joyfully with fewer possessions and greater generosity, we will feel a greater connection with God and the world around us. We will discover with Clare the importance of living simply so that others can simply live.

4

THE TALE OF TWO PRAYERS

The Christmas spirit is transformational. Scrooge learns the joy of generosity. The Grinch's heart grows by three sizes. O. Henry's financially strapped young couple both sell their prized possessions to bring joy to their beloved. A miracle of love happens on 34th Street, and George Bailey learns the true value of his life.

When Francis built the first Christmas creche, his intent was for ordinary people to also be transformed as they were invited to enter the Christmas story. He believed the oft-forgotten masses of humankind were God's beloveds and could claim their vocation as God's messengers in daily life. He saw Infinity where others saw poverty. He saw Beauty where the elite saw ordinariness.

Seeing themselves as Francis and Clare saw them, as loved by God, inspired a new sense of self-agency among the common folk. They realized they not only mattered to Francis and Clare, but they also mattered to God. This meant changing their lives and value systems. It also challenged them to serve God in all their relationships, including their work and citizenship, in ways that would eventually transform the structure of European society. Encountering God always reveals a transformational vision and the invitation to be God's companions in repairing the world.

Visionary moments open us to novel possibilities. A friend, a retired university professor, recently brought to my attention that instead of typing "Acts of the Apostles," I keyboarded "Acts of the Possibles"; typographical errors can be illuminating! The Book of Acts is the account of Christ's followers discovering amazing new possibilities.

As the magnet my mother placed on our refrigerator door, during my childhood years, proclaims, "Prayer changes things." Yes, prayer does change things: first, ourselves and then the world around us. Prayer injects new possibilities that can change cells as well as souls. Prayer can even transform social structures as the American Civil Rights movement demonstrated. Prayer brings peace, but it can also lead to protest. Two prayers, both connected with St. Francis and congruent with the spirit of Clare, can change your life and transform your world.

Although it is unlikely that Francis penned the prayer popularly known as "The Prayer of St. Francis," this prayer does reflect the spirit of the twelfth-century saint:

> *Lord, make me an instrument of Your peace;*
> *Where there is hatred, let me sow love;*
> *Where there is injury, pardon;*
> *Where there is doubt, faith;*
> *Where there is despair, hope;*
> *Where there is darkness, light;*
> *And where there is sadness, joy.*
> *O Divine Master,*
> *Grant that I may not so much seek*
> *To be consoled as to console;*

To be understood, as to understand;
To be loved, as to love;
For it is in giving that we receive,
It is in pardoning that we are pardoned,
And it is in dying that we are born to Eternal Life.

Most mornings I awaken with two affirmations: "This is the day God has made and I will rejoice and be glad in it" (Psalm 118:24) and "Lord, make me an instrument of your peace." Invoking these prayers sets my day in the right direction: gratitude, joy, peace, and agency in doing something beautiful for God wherever I am. The "Franciscan" prayer invites us to loving action in our relationships. Recognizing the profound interdependence of life, this prayer encourages us to choose to go from self-interest and individualism to world loyalty and to compassionate community. When we concern ourselves with the well-being of others consoling, forgiving, bringing light, and hope—we become the artists of our lives and the rebuilders of our communities and the soul of the nation. This prayer reminds us that we are not victims of our personal history or the world in which we live. Instead, we can choose peace and healing in every situation. In the words of Victor Frankl, written out of his experiences in a Nazi concentration camp, "Everything can be taken from a [hu]man but one thing: the last of the human freedoms—to choose one's attitude in any given set of circumstances, to choose one's own way."

Francis's and Clare's lives demonstrate that although we cannot change the circumstances of our birth and social situation, we *can* change our attitudes and broaden our scope of concern to embrace the whole Earth. Our privilege can support protest and activism to change the world. Francis and Clare recognized that while self-interest inspires fear and defensiveness and greed leads to violence, peace broadens our spirits and enables us to live in a world where we are all kinfolk, and where boundaries of friend and foe no longer exist. In creating the first Christmas creche, Francis invited peasants, whose lives were often short and difficult, to see themselves as holy people who could bring beauty and healing to the world one simple action at a time.

During the Christmas season of 2021, I noticed a variation of the Prayer of St. Francis, described as the "Reverse Peace Prayer." This anonymously written prayer, despite its title as the "reverse" of the Prayer of St. Francis, complements the prayer attributed to Francis. Written, I believe, in response to the growing racism, incivility, and attack on human rights in the United States, this prayer calls for bold action. It invites us to picket and pray, and then pray and protest. It invites us to see peacemaking as activist and provocative, not passive.

Franciscan spirituality has gently and persistently challenged injustice in the church and the world. Francis's non-confrontational approach presented a prophetic alternative to the opulence of the Roman church and the economic plight of the ordinary people. In choosing the simplicity of Jesus' birth and life, Francis shined a light on the injustices and prejudices of his time. He dreamed of a world in which everyone was at the center of God's love and the circle of God's love included all creation. This radical vision of human and nonhuman solidarity mandated personal and social transformation. I believe Francis would have been comfortable with the alteration of another well-known prayer, often attributed to activist Angela Davis: "I am no longer accepting the things I cannot change. I am changing the things I cannot accept." I am sure the author of the Serenity Prayer, theologian Reinhold Niebuhr, would also endorse Davis's revision.

The Christmas stories disturb as well as comfort and challenge as well as console. Divine incarnation in a humble stable or cave, among the "nuisances and nobodies of society," as John Dominic Crossan avers, confronts every injustice and humiliation with the light of truth and the call to healing. The Christmas creche inspires our quest to remodel, repair, and rebuild the world. As you travel the Twelve Days of Christmas with Clare, Francis, Jesus, his parents, shepherds, and magic, may your prayers console and disturb, and take you beyond presents and parties to world loyalty and holy restlessness.

> **Lord, make me a channel of disturbance.**
> **Where there is apathy, let me provoke.**
> **Where there is compliance,**
> **let me bring questioning.**
> **Where there is silence, may I be a voice.**
> **Where there is too much comfort**
> **and too little action,**
> **grant disruption.**
> **Where there are doors closed**
> **and hearts locked,**
> **grant the willingness to listen.**
> **When laws dictate and pain is overlooked,**
> **grant that I may rather seek to DO justice**
> **than to TALK about it,**
> **to BE WITH as well as FOR the poor,**
> **to love the unlovable as well as the lovely.**
> **LORD, MAKE ME A CHANNEL OF DISTURBANCE.**

THE TWELVE DAYS
OF CHRISTMAS

CHRISTMAS DAY
DECEMBER 25

All things came into being
through the Word and Wisdom of God,
and without it not one thing
came into being.
What has come into being in him was life,
and the life was the light of all people.
The light shines in the darkness,
and the darkness did not overcome it.

—John 1:2–3

Most high, glorious God,
Enlighten the darkness of my heart,
And give me, Lord, a correct faith,
A certain hope, a perfect charity,
Sense and knowledge, so I may carry out
Your holy and true command.

– Francis of Assisi

C hristmas is the season of light. Christ is the light of the
world, enlightening all. In that light, we see the light
and become lights to others. In Christ's light, shining in
the heavens and in the manger, we see the light and find
our way.

At the same time, darkness can be just as transformative as light. While some people equate darkness with
evil, darkness is also a place of growth: the womb, the soil,
the peaceful night, the starry heavens, the place of dreams
and possibilities, deep space giving birth to the light of
creation. Given the realities of racism, our use of darkness
in our theological reflections should never, in a literal fash-
ion, be related to moral or spiritual evil. The poet Henry
Vaughan recognized the power of Divine darkness to heal
our spirits.

There is in God, some say,
A deep but dazzling darkness; as [humans] here
Say it is late and dusky, because they
See not all clear.
O for that night! where I in Him
Might live invisible and dim!

Still, we all need to be enlightened, in the sense that we need to see with clarity. We need light to find our way through the dimness of our lives. We need the warmth of the sun. We need to be lights to those around us, helping them discern the path they should take.

Today, we need the Solstice light, the emerging light that assures us, as the fourteenth-century mystic Julian of Norwich asserts, that "all shall be well, and all shall be well, and all manner of things shall be well." We need the light that spreads rays of hope on the future, despite the challenges we face as a nation and as a planet.

Francis constantly sought enlightenment. He understood that conversion is not a one-time event but a continuous process, and he was aware of the dimness, confusion, and fear that plagued his spirit. He struggled with his attitudes toward lepers and, no doubt, during the time of the Crusades, wrestled with his prejudice in relation to the Muslim enemy. Perhaps, he faced his anger at a church whose leaders lived lavishly while others were sunk in poverty and malnutrition. Nevertheless, the saint from Assisi and his spiritual companion Clare sought daily to see more deeply into God's incarnation in a Bethlehem hovel, and in that incarnational vision, to see God's presence in every creature, most especially those with whom he felt personal or ethical distance. He knew that when we see the light that shines in us and all things, we can be lights to one another, safe and secure wherever the journey takes us.

> **God of shining light and dazzling darkness,**
> **enlighten my spirit and transform my vision,**
> **that I might be guided by your Way, Truth, and Life.**
> **By your grace, let me shine healing light**
> **on places of chaos and misery;**
> **discern the difference between truth and falsehood;**
> **and share light with fellow pilgrims on the way**
> **that together we might illumine and heal the world.**

THE SECOND DAY OF CHRISTMAS

DECEMBER 26

In the sixth month the angel Gabriel was sent by God to a town in Galilee called Nazareth, to a virgin engaged to a man whose name was Joseph, of the house of David. The virgin's name was Mary.

And he came to her and said, "Greetings, favored one! The Lord is with you." But she was much perplexed by his words and pondered what sort of greeting this might be. The angel said to her, "Do not be afraid, Mary, for you have found favor with God. And now, you will conceive in your womb and bear a son, and you will name him Jesus."... Mary said to the angel, "How can this be, since I am a virgin?" The angel said to her, "The Holy Spirit will come upon you, and the power of the Most High will overshadow you; therefore the child to be born will be holy; he will be called Son of God."... Then Mary said, "Here am I, the servant of the Lord; let it be with me according to your word." Then the angel departed from her.

— Luke 1:26–31, 34–35, 38

We become what we love
and who we love shapes what we become.
We are to become vessels
of God's compassionate love for others.

— Saint Clare

Francis heard God's call when he was alone, kneeling in prayer. Although he may not have completely understood what God was saying to him, he was quick to respond as best he could. Clare heard God's call as she listened to Francis preach—and she responded with a heart full of eagerness and love.

The call of God comes to us in many ways. God is always whispering in our ears, and when we listen to the dramatic or undramatic calls of God, discerned in mystical experiences and ordinary epiphanies, our lives are transformed.

A messenger of God came to young Mary with an amazing request. Perhaps Gabriel had visited other young, more sophisticated and educated young women, who chose not to respond to the Divine call; perhaps they did not notice the angelic presence, disregarded it as inconvenient, or simply said "no." In contrast, Mary said, "Yes." This was not the result, I believe, of her supernatural birth or immaculate conception, free of lust or sin, nor did it depend on Mary's moral perfection. One with us in every way, Mary nevertheless said, "Yes," as the result of her lifelong openness to God's presence, whether in the everyday events of life or in heart-stopping visionary experiences. When Mary said, "Yes," the whole world changed.

An unlikely recipient of Divine revelation, Francis also said, "Yes." At a crossroads in his life, Francis goes to a dilapidated chapel a mile down the hill from Assisi and asks for Divine guidance. A voice calls to him, "Repair my church," and Francis responds affirmatively. Initially, taking God's call literally, Francis repairs the broken walls of the chapel of San Damiano and two other chapels in the vicinity of Assisi. Eventually, he discovers that God's call is global: to repair and reinvigorate the church as a whole and to call the church back to its gospel roots, to establish ministries dedicated to the simple pathway of Jesus and his hospitality to all people, regardless of economics or social standing. Francis's calling was in the spirit of the Jewish spiritual mandate, *tikkun olam*—repair the world. Centuries before the Protestant reformer Martin Luther, Francis discovered that the "reformed church is always reforming." New life and light need to be embraced by each new generation.

Nearly eight centuries after Francis, United Nations General Secretary Dag Hammarskjold in his book *Markings* described his experience of call: "I don't know Who—or what—put the question. I don't know when it was put. I don't even remember answering. But at some moment I did answer *Yes* to Someone—or something—and from that hour I was certain that existence is meaningful and, that, therefore, my life, in self-surrender, had a goal. From that moment I have known what it means 'not to look back' and 'to take no thought for the morrow.'" When we say "yes" to God's call, joining our gifts with the world's needs, we become partners with God in healing the Earth. We become midwives of Christ's birth in the world.

Christmas is the season of saying "yes" to possibility as well as embracing Divine invitations that, prior to God's call, we defined as impossibilities. The magic of the season requires the catalyst of our willingness to embrace new and seemingly impossible possibilities. Like Mary, Francis, Clare, and Hammarskjold, we will discover amazing new insights and adventures with the infant and growing Jesus as our companion.

Help me, God of impossibilities,
to discover that nothing is impossible with you.
Help me to be attentive to your call in my life,
the call of big things as well as the call
emerging in ordinary moments.
Give me the grace to say "yes"
to what appears to be currently
beyond my capabilities and the courage
to become more than I imagined
as I commit to being your companion
in repairing the world.

THE THIRD DAY OF CHRISTMAS

DECEMBER 27

Now the birth of Jesus the Messiah took place in this way. When his mother Mary had been engaged to Joseph, but before they lived together, she was found to be with child from the Holy Spirit. Her husband Joseph, being a righteous man and unwilling to expose her to public disgrace, planned to dismiss her quietly.

But just when he had resolved to do this, an angel of the Lord appeared to him in a dream and said, "Joseph, son of David, do not be afraid to take Mary as your wife, for the child conceived in her is from the Holy Spirit. She will bear a son, and you are to name him Jesus, for he will save his people from their sins." . . . When Joseph awoke from sleep, he did as the angel of the Lord commanded him; he took her as his wife.

— Matthew 1:18–21, 24

A voice spoke to Francis, "Who can do more good, the master or the servant?"

"The master," he answered.

"Then why are you looking for the servant, rather than the master?"

"Ah! Lord, what would you have me do?"

"Return home, and there you will learn what is right for you to do. The vision that you had in a dream, you must interpret in a completely new way"

— from Francis's first biography, written by one of his followers, Thomas of Celano.

REPAIRING THE WORLD

Although the young Francis of Assisi sought to become a nobleman through performing valorous acts, he was a failure as a knight. When his side was defeated, he was captured and imprisoned; after being released from prison, Francis decided to join another military troop, hoping to prove his bravery as a stepping stone to nobility. Convalescing from illness and depressed that his companions went ahead without him, Francis was again the recipient of a Divine message, challenging him to use his resources, gifts, and experiences on behalf of Jesus' realm rather than an earthly ruler.

Theologian Paul Tillich described faith in terms of "ultimate concern," our commitment to a reality that promises supreme fulfillment and asks for absolute sacrifice. In today's readings, we discover that both Francis and Joseph were, by implication, presented with the questions: "What is your ultimate concern? Earthly success? Financial security? Good health? Reputation? Fulfilling your culture's value system? Or does your ultimate concern involve trusting God to provide the vision and resources to do God's will and fulfill your destiny, regardless of the challenges you will have to face? Do you trust God to make a way when you see no way forward?"

Mysticism leads to action. Encountering God always challenges us to reevaluate our prior goals and realign our values—and the twelve days of Christmas give us an opportunity to step back from our busy lives and listen for God's voice. The focus on relationships and generosity during the Christmas season invites us to reflect on what is truly important to us: love or success, compassion or self-interest, generosity or materialism, forgiveness or alienation. Francis and Joseph both learned that following God's vision involves the interplay of personal fulfillment and care for others. When we follow the Spirit, solutions to life's problems emerge, and we discover as did Francis and Joseph that a way forward appears where once we saw only a dead end.

The angel reassured both Mary and Joseph with the promise, "Don't be afraid." Francis also needed to hear that counsel when he left his life of consumerism and upward mobility to follow the uncharted pathway, simply living with Jesus as his guide. We need to hear these same words— "Don't be afraid"—as we explore new values, behaviors, and lifestyles, letting go of familiar patterns to embrace the road that lies before us.

Adventurous and challenging God,
confront my complacency. Contest my values.
Undermine habits that no longer serve me
and those around me, so that I may discover
what is truly important in life.
Reassure me in times of transition.
Remind me that in sacrificing the unimportant,
I will receive gifts beyond belief
and the opportunity to be your companion
in bringing love and beauty to the world.

THE FOURTH DAY
OF CHRISTMAS

DECEMBER 28

And she gave
birth to her
firstborn son
and wrapped him
in bands of cloth,
and laid him
in a manger,
because there
was no place for
them in the inn.

—Luke 2:7

Consider,
contemplate,
as you desire to imitate.

—Saint Clare

In her letter to the Princess Agnes of Bohemia, Clare advised her to gaze upon Christ in his humility, and then deepen her gaze by internalizing Christ's spirit so that she might imitate Christ's way. To do this, Clare, like Francis immersed, herself in the senses. Both Clare and Francis lived simply and frugally, especially by today's standards. But they were also mystics of the five senses, for whom God was found in the most ordinary of encounters as well as the majestic heavens above.

A child in a manger, surrounded by farm animals, and attracting shepherds weary from their nocturnal labors, reveals the heart of God. These "essential" employees saw more than an ordinary baby. The hymns of angelic messengers opened their senses to God incarnate in a little child. The magic of Christmas was found then, as today, in the delightful interplay of sight, sound, smell, taste, and touch.

Today, we delight in the simple pageants with children and adults gathered in the sanctuary and acting out the Nativity of Jesus. We rejoice in hearing familiar carols, and we anticipate the aroma of Christmas dinner and the taste of cakes and cookies. The fragrance of incense centers our spirits and invests the simplest of spaces with holiness. Memories of snowballs, chilled in our hands, and the snowball fights that often ensued, take us back to childhood and tempt us to launch a snowball at an unsuspecting grandchild. A hug from a child or a dear friend, especially after a long absence due to the pandemic, fills the yearning to embrace a God with skin.

The world is the primary revelation of God, and our senses are portals to eternity. When the doors of perception are cleansed, we view everything as infinite. The amazing beauties of the earth point to the Beauty of Eternity. Time and its changes is the moving image of eternity. With eyes on the Infinite, we discover the finite beauty of daily life.

The child in the manger is Divinity incarnate, and in contemplating Jesus' birth, we encounter God in every child, whether their birth is in a well-equipped maternity ward or a rudimentary shelter, the child of undocumented immigrants on the US borderlands.

With memories of Christmas Day still fresh, take time to gaze upon the faces of Divinity in your neighborhood. Celebrate the ordinary manifestations of God in a child playing with yesterday's Christmas present, the sight of falling snowflakes, the feel of a chill wind on your cheeks, or the warm sunshine reviving your limbs. Inspired by your contemplations, consider how you might imitate God's colorful artistry and midwife the birth of Divinity as you go about your daily adventures.

Awaken my senses to beauty, you who made all beauty.

May the beauties I experience open me

to the Beauty that gives birth to each wondrous day.

With beauty all around,

let me midwife holiness and inspire creativity

imitating in my unique way

the Artist of Creation and Poet of Incarnation.

THE FIFTH DAY OF CHRISTMAS

DECEMBER 29

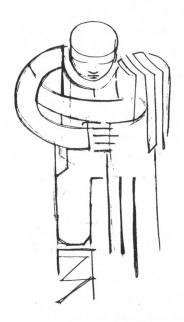

In that region there were shepherds living in the fields, keeping watch over their flock by night. Then an angel of the Lord stood before them, and the glory of the Lord shone around them, and they were terrified. But the angel said to them, "Do not be afraid; for see—I am bringing you good news of great joy for all the people: to you is born this day in the city of David a Savior, who is the Messiah, the Lord. This will be a sign for you: you will find a child wrapped in bands of cloth

and lying in a manger." And suddenly
there was with the angel a multitude of the
heavenly host, praising God and saying,

"Glory to God in the highest heaven,
 and on earth peace among
those whom he favors!"

When the angels had left them and
gone into heaven, the shepherds said to one
another, "Let us go now to Bethlehem and
see this thing that has taken place, which
the Lord has made known to us." ...
The shepherds returned, glorifying and
praising God for all they had heard
and seen, as it had been told them.

— Luke 2:8–15, 20

In the Middle Ages, lepers were considered
the dregs of society. A leper had to shake
a rattle when he moved about in order
to alert healthy people against sudden
encounters .... Francis affirmed, "And in
going about with them, what had seemed
to me bitter was changed for me into
sweetness of the soul and the body."

— from Francis's biography by André Vauchez

REPAIRING THE WORLD

nitially, Francis thoughtlessly embraced his society's fear of lepers. To him, they were repugnant and carried with them the threat of disease and death. But then Francis's vision was transformed. He encountered a person with leprosy on the road, felt his usual revulsion, and then experienced something entirely different—God coming to him in the form of a leper. Francis overcame his fear, embraced and kissed the person with leprosy, and eventually became the patron saint of persons with leprosy. He discovered the face of God, as Mother Teresa affirmed, in all of God's distressing disguises. The light that shined in Bethlehem illuminated the faces of persons with leprosy.

Deep down, most of us have our "lepers," persons we look down upon, view as unclean or beyond the circle of God's love and our ethical consideration. Our outcasts can be defined by race, ethnicity, citizenship status, religion, or politics. During the pandemic, many of us avoided at all costs people who were unvaccinated or refused to wear masks in public places. I must admit I have found it difficult to see the face of God in persons who are anti-science, circulate conspiracy theories, and champion authoritarian images of God. I am tempted to see them and their leaders as ignoramuses, unworthy of my compassion or ethical consideration. Francis's experience with persons with leprosy reminds me that God loves those whose behaviors place them at the margins of my ethical concern. The light of God shines in the darkness, my own and theirs, and each one of us, regardless of our politics or lifestyle is God's beloved child.

In the first century, shepherds were considered outsiders, living at the margins of society. Though they were truly "essential" workers, providing food and wool to the community, their lives were challenging. Despite the romanticized images portrayed in Christmas pageants, their daily life was hard, pay was low, and many were unsheltered, like today's homeless community. And yet shepherds, not royalty, are visited by angels and regaled by the angelic chorus. From now on, after hearing the singing of the angels, they know God loves them, and that they matter, regardless of their place in society. God called, they listened—ran to Bethlehem.

During this Christmas season, reflect on your own spiritual, ethical, and relational outcasts. Consider the impact of your feelings of judgment and alienation on your own spiritual life and upon those you place outside the circle of love. Let the words of Francis's follower, Saint Bonaventure, inspire you to see the holiness of people whose behaviors and politics you challenge: "God is a circle whose center is everywhere and whose circumference is nowhere."

May the Spirit of Christmas guide my path today.
May I see your face in the lost and lonely, Spirit,
in the nuisances and nobodies
of my neighborhood and the planet.
May my compassion embrace those
whose political viewpoints, behaviors,
and attitudes are reprehensible to me.
May I see them as your beloved children,
even when I challenge their viewpoints.

THE SIXTH DAY OF CHRISTMAS

DECEMBER 30

For a child has been
born for us,
a son given to us;
authority rests upon
his shoulders;
and he is named
Wonderful
Counselor,
Mighty God,
Everlasting Father,
Prince of Peace.

—Isaiah 9:6

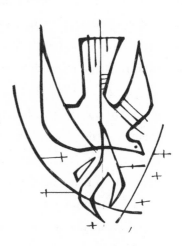

Before he proposed the word of God
to those gathered about, he first
prayed for peace for them, saying,
"The Lord give you peace."
He always announced peace
to all men and women . . . he met.

—from Francis's first biographer, Thomas of Celano

In a time of conflict and dissension between families, feudal lords, and clans, as well as the Crusades against Islam, Francis's words of peace seemed unrealistic. For Francis, peace was the essential message of his calling from God, and it was the guiding principle that gave his life direction. The people of Francis's day, including the clergy, were shocked and uncomfortable with Francis's words and lifestyle. To them, as to us today, the promise of Jesus to his followers sounds like an impossible dream: "Peace I leave with you; my peace I give to you. I do not give to you as the world gives. Do not let your hearts be troubled, and do not let them be afraid" (John 14:27). In a time of unrelenting violence and war, Francis chose to follow the "Prince of Peace," the Child of Bethlehem, whose birth brings joy to the world and hope to humanity.

When Francis went to the Pope, asking for permission to found a religious order, the Pope's first response was to advise Francis to instead become a hermit. Francis asked Clare to pray for God's guidance, and together they realized that the life of the hermit would not allow him to be an active peace-bringer in his troubled world. Violence was interwoven with the very structure of his society, much like it is today. Francis called his followers to be "delegates for peace," and he said to them:

Since you speak of peace, all the more so must you have it in your hearts. Let none be provoked to anger or scandal by you, but rather may they be drawn to peace and good will through your gentleness. We have been called to heal wounds, to unite what has fallen apart, and to bring home those who have lost their way.

Buddhist spiritual guide Thich Nhat Hanh counseled that "peace is every step," and taught a breath prayer that not only eases tension but brings peace to troubled spirits:

Breathing in, I feel calm.
Breathing out, I smile.

A child in Bethlehem, two Italian monastics, and a Vietnamese Buddhist monk—all pave the pathway to peace. In the spirit of Francis, Clare, Jesus, and Thich Nhat Hanh, whenever you meet someone, breathe deeply and smile, blessing each encounter with, "May God give you peace." Your prayers could be the tipping point from conflict to peace and incivility to respect, as you mediate God's vision "on earth as it is in heaven."

Child of Peace,
I accept the peace you give me,
and I commit to being an instrument of your peace.
May I bless everyone I meet with your peace,
sowing seeds of forgiveness, love, reconciliation,
and healing wherever I go.

THE SEVENTH DAY OF CHRISTMAS

DECEMBER 31

The true light, which enlightens everyone,
was coming into the world.

— John 1:9

From the example of Francis, the Sultan
came to understand a ... meaning of the
imitation of Christ.
... From the Sultan,
Frances learned
that Islam wasn't a
religion of violence,
depravity, and hatred,
but was a religion of
spiritual reflection,
intellectual curiosity,
and sincere devotion
to the creator. Via
their open and
honest discourse,

by setting aside the preconceptions
... they came to understand each
other and their religions, thus gifting
later generations an example of the
potential for peace that resided in an
open, honest, and equal discourse.

— Dustin J. Byrd

F rancis was constantly crossing borders. His faith had no
boundaries but was an ever-expanding circle in which enemies became friends and strangers morphed into companions.
He saw God's center everywhere and in every heart. Everyone
was a saint in the making, despite their current waywardness.

In a time of war, Francis became a diplomat for Jesus, taking a dangerous risk by reaching out to the Muslim
Sultan. Death was a real possibility, but Francis knew this
was what Jesus would have done. Jesus had embraced Roman centurions and Jewish religious leaders, as well as unclean lepers, women, and hated tax collectors. Now, for
Francis, as for Jesus, the "other" was not a threat to be feared
but a "holy other" to be loved.

John's Gospel tells us that the true Light enlightens
everyone. There is chaos and sin in our world, and people

routinely go astray, guided by the blindness and selfishness of their hearts. But nevertheless, God's light shines in every heart, and God's aim is for everyone to experience enlightenment.

The Christmas stories are about seeing the light and being the light. They are also about bringing forth the light hidden in others. The light shines in the darkness of the womb and the night sky. "You are the light of the world," Jesus announced to his followers, and that is a promissory note given to all of us.

On this final day of the year, when we need to let go of the past, building on its accomplishments, and repairing its faults, take time to reflect on these questions: What would it mean for you to be a light-bearer? What would it mean for you to open the doors of perception to see the light in a white nationalist, a prevaricating politician, a troublesome relative, or an angry motorist? In what way, might you recognize God's light in yourself, let it shine, and then choose to make room for others to see the light in themselves?

In your light, O God, I see light.
Your light enlightens me and guides my path.
Let your light shine in and through me
so that I may midwife the birthing of your Light
in familiar as well as unfamiliar and challenging places.

REPAIRING THE WORLD

THE EIGHTH DAY OF CHRISTMAS

JANUARY 1

Praise the Lord from the heavens; praise him in the heights! Praise him, all his angels; praise him, all his host! Praise him, sun and moon; praise him, all you shining stars! Praise him, you highest heavens, and you waters above the heavens! Praise the Lord from the earth, you sea monsters and all deeps, fire and hail, snow and frost, stormy wind fulfilling his command!

Mountains and all hills,
fruit trees and all cedars!
Wild animals and all cattle, creeping
things and flying birds!

—Psalm 148:1–4, 7–10

Be praised, my Lord,
through all your creatures,
especially through my lord Brother Sun,
who brings the day;
and you give light through him.
And he is beautiful and
radiant in all his splendor!
Of you, Most High, he bears the likeness.
Praise be you, my Lord,
through Sister Moon
and the stars, in heaven you formed them
clear and precious and beautiful.
Praised be you, my Lord,
through Brother Wind,
and through the air, cloudy and serene,
and every kind of weather through which
you give sustenance to your creatures.
Praised be you, my Lord,
through Sister Water....

Praised be You, my Lord,
through Brother Fire. . . .
Praised be You, my Lord,
through Sister Mother Earth,
who sustains us and governs us.

—Saint Francis

The psalmist, Francis, and Clare welcome us to a new year, inviting us to claim a new vision of reality, the vision of a living and dynamic universe of which we are a part. The psalmist describes a world of praise and summons us to take our place in God's earthly chorus. Francis follows suit, affirming that the sun, the moon, wind and water, fire, and the Earth herself all declare the glory of God. According to Francis's earliest biographer, Thomas of Celano, as Francis was traveling, singing of Jesus as he went, he would often come to a halt in the road, totally forgetting he was traveling toward a particular destination. There he would stand in the road and invite all creatures—birds, trees, flowers, rabbits—to praise Jesus with him. Clare, who called herself "a little plant," was happy to take her humble place amid an entire living universe of praise.

"Joy to the world, the Lord has come—and heaven and nature sing!" Christmas challenges us to go beyond anthropocentrism to visualize Christ not only in the face of a newborn baby, but in the birth of a puppy, pangolin, or panda bear. The cows, sheep, and horses in the creche remind us that the animal world also lives by God's incarnation. God's wise creativity parents a child in Bethlehem, just as God brings forth, in the movements of creation, an orderly and beautiful world, long before humanity's emergence. Our joy at Christ's coming bursts forth in carols as we hear the songs of the humpbacked whale. A world of praise awakens our love for creation and care for the Earth. We are the gardeners and stewards of creation, and the fate of the Earth depends on our willingness to repair her.

Wise and loving Creator,
let creation's praises sound through us.
Let us join the voices of sea, sky, and earth,
of all creatures in a symphony of praise.
Let us, with all creation, praise you.
And let us live more simply so that
creation can simply live,
and the good Earth flourish, bringing
forth bountiful harvests
for our companions, human and non-human alike.
Let heaven and nature ring!

THE NINTH DAY
OF CHRISTMAS

JANUARY 2

Look at the birds of the air; they neither sow nor reap nor gather into barns, and yet your heavenly Father feeds them. Are you not of more value than they? And can any of you by worrying add a single hour to your span of life? And why do you worry about clothing? Consider the lilies of the field,

how they grow; they neither toil nor
spin, yet I tell you, even Solomon in all his
glory was not clothed like one of these.

—Matthew 6:26–29

My brother birds, you should greatly praise
your Creator, and love him always. He
gave you feathers to wear, wings to fly, and
whatever you need. God made you noble
among His creatures and gave you a home
in the purity of the air, so that you neither
sow nor reap, He nevertheless protects
and governs you without the least care.

—Francis's sermon to the birds

As Francis was traveling with his brothers, he saw a huge
flock of birds—doves, crows, and grackles—roosting in
a field near the road. Francis left his followers and ran across
the field, where he greeted the birds in his usual way: "The
Lord give you peace!" To his surprise, the birds did not fly
away, and so he asked them humbly if they would listen to the
Word of God. Thomas of Celano, Francis's first biographer
and one of his first followers, said that when Francis had
finished his sermon,

the birds rejoiced in a wonderful way according to their nature. They stretched their necks, spread their wings, opened their beaks and looked at him. He passed through their midst, coming and going, touching their heads and bodies with his tunic. Then he blessed them, and having made the sign of the cross, gave them permission to fly off to another place. . . . From that day on, he carefully exhorted all birds, all animals, all reptiles, and also insensible creatures, to praise and love the Creator, because daily, invoking the name of the Savior, he observed their obedience in his own experience.

Francis believed that the human and nonhuman alike experience both the joys and sorrows of life, reflect God's care, and have the vocation of praising their Creator. Humans are not alone in a meaningless universe: we share the world with an amazing plentitude of creatures, each with its own gift and place in the totality of life.

The nonhuman world is touched by God and can respond faithfully to God's call. Sparrows, fish, and donkeys are attentive to Divine wisdom. From this understanding of the universe, Francis befriended the wolf of Gubbio and brokered peace between the wolf and the villagers.

According to legend, Jesus' birth took place in a cave or a stable, surrounded by cattle, sheep, chickens, and a donkey. His birth is announced by a star. Surely the coming of Christ reflects the words of another hymn: "All nature sings and around me rings the music of the spheres. . . . The morning light, the lily white, declare their Maker's praise."

Francis lived in an enchanted world—a joyous symphony in which every creature could burst forth in praise, sharing wisdom with its human kin. Today, Francis invites us to enter that world; to do so, we must balance our technological achievements with care for our planet. For countless ages, animals have faithfully cared for humans and given their lives so that humans can eat—and humans must care for the nonhuman world.

Today, as we embrace the wonder of this Earth, may we pause to contemplate a pigeon, a leaf, a caterpillar, or a tree.

In beauty may I walk.
All day long may I walk.
Through the returning seasons may I walk.
On the trail marked with pollen may I walk.
With grasshoppers about my feet may I walk.
With dew about my feet may I walk. . . .
With Beauty before me may I walk.
With Beauty behind me may I walk.
With Beauty above me may I walk.
With Beauty beneath my feet may I walk.
With Beauty all around me may I walk.
In old age wandering on a trail of Beauty,
Living again may I walk.
All is completed in Beauty.
—*Navaho prayer*

THE TENTH DAY OF CHRISTMAS

JANUARY 3

And she gave birth
to her firstborn son
and wrapped him
in bands of cloth,
and laid him in
a manger,
because there
was no place for
them in the inn.

—Luke 2:7

O Blessed Poverty,
who bestows
eternal riches
on those who love
and embrace her!
O Holy Poverty, to
those who possess
and desire you,

God promises the kingdom of heaven,
and offers, indeed, eternal
glory and blessed life.
O God-centered poverty, whom
the Lord Jesus Christ . . .
who spoke and things were made,
condescended to embrace.

—Saint Clare

Following the pathway of Jesus, both Clare and Francis chose to divest themselves from their possessions to live fully dependent upon Divine Providence. "What a great laudable exchange," wrote Clare, "to leave the things of time for those of eternity."

In the Letter to the Philippians, the Apostle Paul counseled the emerging Christian community at Philippi to have the same mind as Jesus who "emptied himself, taking the form of a slave, being born in human likeness." Francis and Clare believed that authentic fulfillment comes from following Jesus' example, letting go of everything that stands in the way of our relationship with God.

The church authorities, however, were not happy about Clare and Francis's insistence on absolute poverty for their followers. Some people thought they were simply being impractical, while wealthier church officials resented the implied criticism of their lifestyle.

Today, simplicity is still countercultural, especially during the "season of giving," which has become identified with profit-making and consumption. We wear ourselves out looking for the perfect gift, spending hours online and at stores. Sabbath time with family is eclipsed by busyness, and the graceful spirit of Christmas and the simplicity of the Holy Family is forgotten. The humble birth of Jesus shows us, though, that true fulfillment comes not from what we own but from our relationships with God and the human and nonhuman beings with whom we share our world.

Today, despite our relative economic well-being (compared to those who truly suffer poverty), many of us are dissatisfied. We are possessed by our possessions. We are anxious in our affluence and plagued by our prosperity. Perhaps we need to practice spiritual as well as material decluttering to experience the abundant life God longs to give us.

Clare and Francis did not glorify involuntary poverty. They felt the pain of the homeless and dispossessed. Their hearts were broken by the ostracism of people with leprosy and the faces of hungry children. I believe that in today's world, Francis and Clare would be at the forefront of advocacy for economic justice and health care, as well as environmental justice and healing. Their poverty was a choice, reflecting both their calling to depend on Christ and Christ alone, and their solidarity with those who were experiencing the world's oppression and injustice.

Let us remember in this Christmas season what is truly important: loving families, good friends, shared bounty with those who need it most, and joyful memories that last a lifetime—and let us work for a world in which our privileges are shared by all our kin.

> **Loving God, like the baby born in a manger,**
> **let us trust your love and the love of**
> **others for our true happiness.**
> **Let our hearts be warmed by generosity**
> **as we embody the spirit of Christmas in joyful sacrifice.**
> **Let our spirits expand to embrace**
> **the lonely and forgotten.**
> **Let us put your Realm of Love first**
> **as we proclaim God's peace to everyone we meet.**

THE ELEVENTH DAY
OF CHRISTMAS

JANUARY 4

But to all who received him,
who believed in his name,
he gave power to become children of God,
who were born, not of blood
or of the will of the flesh
or of the will of man, but of God.
And the Word became flesh
and lived among us,

and we have seen his glory,
the glory as of a father's only
son, full of grace and truth.

—John 1:12–14

Place your mind before the
mirror of eternity!
Place your soul in the brilliance of glory.
Place your heart in the figure
of divine substance.
And transform your whole being
into the image of Godhead itself
through contemplation,
so that you may feel what his friends feel
as they taste the hidden sweetness
which God himself has reserved
from the very beginning
for those who love him.

—Saint Clare

Jesus was born in the fullness of time, to bring healing to our world. He was born into a world not so different from ours today, a world where many people suffered because of oppression, injustice, violence, and poverty. Jesus never spent a moment of his life enjoying the freedoms persons in democracies enjoy; he and his fellow Jews had their "backs against the wall," to quote theologian Howard Thurman. The threat of violence, like the violence of the South in the Jim Crow era and in dictatorships today, lay waiting barely beneath the surface of any encounter with Caesar's occupation force.

Jesus' solidarity with the poor and the oppressed continues to show everyday people and people at the margins that they are God's beloved children, worthy of respect and capable of changing themselves and the world. When John's Gospel says, "God so loved the world," it means God loves *everyone*—you, me, those who are close to us and those who believe differently than we do, those we love and those we dislike, as well as our pets and farm animals, wild creatures, and every inhabitant of our planet, from the smallest one-celled creature to the greatest blue whale.

Following the spirit of John's Gospel, Clare and Francis carried this love into the world; Francis did this by traveling far and near, preaching his message of peace, while Clare did her part from within the cloister of her convent. Both of them experienced the true power of sacrificing everything for the gospel. They found meaning and purpose and a voice that still speaks to us today. They discovered that nothing can ever separate us from the love of God, and in downward mobility, they experienced abundant life. Their lives remind us that we are truly empowered when we embrace the Christmas spirit. God is not only with us but also in us, and we are tasked with showing that love to others, as Clare and Francis did. The humble birth of Jesus inspires abundant life now and forevermore.

Help me, Jesus, to focus on your presence in all creation
that I might love you in heart, mind, and soul.
Let me be your hands and feet
in bringing joy to the world and healing to the nation.
May I have the infinite hope that will empower me
to live courageously, despite finite disappointments.

THE TWELFTH DAY OF CHRISTMAS

JANUARY 5

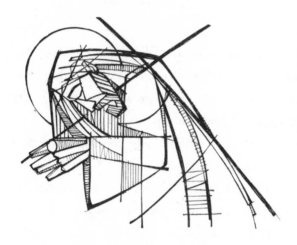

For God so loved the world
that he gave his only Son,
so that everyone who believes
in him may not perish
but may have eternal life.

—John 3:16

Praised be you
through our Sister Bodily Death,
from whom no one living can escape.
Praise and bless my Lord, and give
Him thanks
and serve Him with great humility.

—Saint Francis

Unlike many of today's holiday revelers, Francis and Clare recognized that the reality of death lurks in the background of the Christmas stories. As Rome's representative, Herod ruled Judea with an iron fist, and when he heard of the birth of a new spiritual leader, he wanted to eliminate any competition to his rule. Warned by a dream, Joseph fled with his family to Egypt. Jesus' life was saved, but Herod's fearful lust for power left in its wake the massacre of the innocents.

Francis's "Canticle" concludes with the affirmation that death itself can be an instrument of grace. Our response to death can be an opportunity to praise God. Even as his life ebbed, Francis praised God for the gift of life.

In fact, he and his companions had a festival of hymn-singing so loud that one of his followers rebuked him, saying that such gleeful singing on death's door could set a bad example for the laity. Francis and his friends continued to sing, however, full-throated and joyfully, joining with Brother Sun and Sister Moon, the wolf of Gubbio, and countless lepers and birds in praising God. Francis, like the apostle Paul, knew that "neither angels nor demons, neither the present nor the future, nor any powers, neither height nor depth, nor anything else in all creation, will be able to separate us from the love of God that is in Christ Jesus our Lord" (Romans 8:38–39). And like Paul, Francis believed that "for to me, living is Christ and dying is gain" (Philippians 1:21). He knew that the One who companioned him on the pilgrimage of life, who guided his path and expanded his vision, would be waiting for him at the hour of death.

The Christmas message is that God is with us in every season of life, perhaps especially when we find ourselves weak and powerless. God became human so that we might become divine, and in living in every season from birth to death, Jesus defined all the seasons of life as holy.

After a series of health crises left Dorothy Day unable to travel for speaking engagements or to protest injustice, she remarked, "My vocation is now simply to pray." This is good advice for people with diminished health, whether from long COVID or some other chronic illness, and it is also sensible counsel for the elders among us (and the elders in the making, like those of us in the Medicare generation).

We always have value when we can pray for the world and those around us!

As I grow older, I give thanks for every new day. Each day is a blessing, and I know that all the days to come are opportunities for me to praise God and love the people around me. With that attitude, I embrace the spirit of Francis and Clare, knowing that I too can choose to be God's companion in healing the world.

Loving God, help me experience your loving wisdom
in every season of life.
Help me to know that whether I live or die,
I belong to you, and you have plans for me,
plans for a future with hope.
Let the reality of death inspire me
to live each day fully, claiming my role
as a good ancestor to future generations.
May I do something beautiful for you
in all my encounters.

THE EPIPHANY OF JESUS
JANUARY 6

After they had heard the king, they went on their way, and the star they had seen when it rose went ahead of them until it stopped over the place where the child was. When they saw the star, they were overjoyed. On coming to the house, they saw the child with his mother Mary, and they bowed down and worshiped him. Then they opened their treasures and presented him with gifts of gold, frankincense and myrrh. And having been warned in a dream not to go back to Herod, they returned to their country by another route.

— Matthew 2:9–12

Almighty, eternal, just and merciful God, . . .
inwardly cleansed, interiorly enlightened,
and inflamed by the power
of the Holy Spirit,
may we be able to follow in the footprints
of Your beloved Son, our Lord Jesus Christ.

—Saint Francis

The magi came from the East. Most likely, they were Zoroastrians, followers of the Persian holy man Zarathustra, who challenged his followers to side with the Divine light in the struggle against moral evil. Today, these magi would likely have come from Iran, a nation whose leaders—not the Iranian people—are in conflict with the United States. The magi's Iranian origins remind us that God's light shines everywhere, including in the lives of those we are tempted to define as enemies.

One of my favorite verses in scripture relates to the journey of the magi: "They returned to their country by another route." Life is full of detours and roads not taken, and other roads claimed. We often think life will take us in this direction—and discover ourselves on an entirely different route. My goal was to be a seminary president, but I ended my professional career pastoring a historic church on Cape Cod.

Looking at my life as a totality, I thank God each day for the roads not taken, as well as for the path I took. I thought I would spend my retirement years walking the beaches of Cape Cod, and now I am living in the Washington, DC, suburbs, two miles from my grandchildren. I miss the beach but being a good ancestor to two growing boys is my vocation, and I am grateful. Every day is filled with promise and unexpected turns. I am grateful for the unexpected blessings I have received and the dead ends that gave way to new horizons.

For me, the culmination of the Christmas season is the Feast of Epiphany. Epiphany brings Christ to the world, unplugged, untrammeled, unbounded, and unlimited. Epiphany is the season of universal revelation. The baby in the manger can now be found everywhere, for Christ is bigger than Christmas and, for that matter, Christianity. Christ is the reality "in whom we live and move and have our being" (Act17:28). Confronted by what theologian Thomas Jay Oord calls the "uncontrolling love of God," we discover that the power of love is more essential than the love of power. Francis reminds us the whole Earth is an epiphany, every place is transparent to Divinity, and every newborn baby is a revelation of God.

The universality of the Epiphany season keeps the Christmas spirit alive. The twelve days of Christmas can morph into a lifetime, and each day can be filled with wonder, as we sojourn with Francis, Clare, and the Child who grew up to be our Companion and Guidepost on every adventure.

And so, let us go into the new year, filled with the Christmas Spirit as we celebrate the Epiphany of love, with Clare's blessing: "May the Lord be with you always and, wherever you are, be with Him always."

**Holy Adventurer, loving Companion,
sojourn with me.
Let me follow the path you have set before me.
Let my footprints be found alongside yours,
creating my own path
with you as my guide and friend.
When I travel unexpected roads,
let me trust that all roads lead to you
and that angels guide my steps.
With each footstep, draw me closer to your Home;
guide me by your vision and inspire me
to join hands with all my companions
on this good Earth.**

More inspiration for
the Christmas season
and beyond . . .

THE WORK OF CHRISTMAS
The 12 Days of Christmas
with Howard Thurman

This book is a celebration of the twelve days of Christmas, offering us a chance to dwell on the meaning of the season in dialogue with the wisdom of one of America's greatest mystics and activists, Howard Thurman.

During the twelve days of Christmas, our goal is to experience God's light, despite the temptation to close our hearts in a world too often characterized by racism, sexism, polarization, nationalism, and exclusion. This season asks us instead

to open our hearts and our lives, so that throughout the year ahead, we may be light-bearers, carrying the message of Divine justice and hope, making it come alive even in the darkest corners of the world. This is the year-round work of Christmas!

I WONDER AS I WANDER
The 12 Days of Christmas
with Madeleine L'Engle

How can we recover the radical meaning of the Christmas season? Using the thoughts and words of Madeleine L'Engle, this books offers you a guide through the hectic Christmas season. With quiet times of prayer, Scripture, and meditation, you can begin to wonder—to imagine big possibilities and ask important questions—as you wander outside your typical comfort zones. In the twelve days of Christmas, bookended by Christmas Eve and the Feast of Epiphany, you will experience anew the awe and wonder of the Incarnation.

As you both wonder and wander, the questions and images in this book will open your heart to the radical message of Christmas.

THIN PLACES EVERYWHERE
The 12 Days of Christmas with Celtic Christianity

Bruce Epperly invites you to share a Christmas adventure with him, voyaging through the 12 days of Christmas (plus Christmas Eve and Epiphany) with Brendan, Columba, Brigid, Patrick, and other Celtic saints. With these Celtic adventurers as your companions, you will discover "thin places"—moments of time when the Incarnation of Christ shines through ordinary people, places, and events. After the busyness of Advent, the days that follow Christmas can be a quieter time, when you can venture out on an inner vision quest for new ways of seeing and being.

May your Christmas journey awaken you to thin places everywhere.

BECOME FIRE!
GUIDEPOSTS FOR INTERSPIRITUAL PILGRIMS

In the spirit of God's call to creative transformation, Bruce Epperly invites you to join him on a holy adventure in spiritual growth, inspired by the evolving wisdom of Christianity and the world's great spiritual traditions, innovative global spiritual practices, and emerging visions of reality. Epperly explores the many resources of Christian spirituality in dialogue with the spiritual practices of the world's great wisdom traditions, describing the gifts other spiritu-

al paths contribute to the pathway of Jesus; at the same time, he uses the lens of the spiritual practices Jesus has inspired throughout Christian history to examine these spiritual paths.

Cosmos to Cradle
Meditations on the Incarnation

This book takes its inspiration from the familiar Gospel Nativity stories—but it is far more than a Christmas book. As we revisit the characters of the familiar Christmas stories, we are invited to a new understanding of the Incarnation. We realize that, like Mary, we too are called to be the wombs and midwives of Divine revelation. We may receive Divine guidance and inspiration in dreams, just as Joseph did, and like him, find the courage to go against our society's expectations. Like the shepherds, we are welcomed to see the ongoing glorious pageant of God-made-flesh. And finally, we learn from the magis' example to widen our spiritual horizons and explore new paths.

In Jesus, the Word is made flesh; God has skin, cells, a reproductive system, and circulatory system. Our own souls and cells also reveal God's artistry, for they too embody the Source of all life. In fact, incarnation is everywhere we turn, revealing the marriage of Creator and creature in all its messiness.

SANTA CLAUS
Saint, Shaman, & Symbol

If you don't believe in Santa, you might want to reconsider. The familiar fellow dressed in red has been around a lot longer than the malls' Santa, longer than Rudolph, longer even than "The Night Before Christmas." His earliest and most ancient forms brought hope and cheer to generation after generation of humankind—and he still has a message for us today. In the midst of the materialism of the modern

holiday, Santa offers us a bridge between the physical, secular world and the spiritual, sacred realm. Discover his history and evolution, from Ice Age shaman to medieval saint to modern-day icon. Get to know Santa— and believe all over again.

Prepare the Way
Celtic Prayers for the Season of Light

Ray Simpson has given his life, both professionally and personally, to Celtic Christianity, and now he helps us to celebrate a Celtic outlook on the season of Christmas. With their eloquent yet simple words, his prayers welcome the Holy One who comes to us in small, ordinary ways, who is present in the helpless and the vulnerable. As we join Ray in prayer, we stand on the threshold to paradox and mystery—and we "prepare the way" for God to enter our world anew.

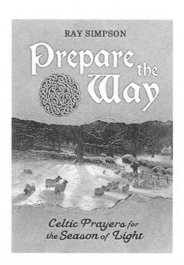

BRUCE EPPERLY has served as a seminary professor and administrator, university chaplain, and congregational pastor. An ordained minister with the United Church of Christ and Christian Church (Disciples of Christ), he is the author of more than sixty books, including *From Cosmos to Cradle: Meditations on the Incarnation* and *The Elephant is Running: Process and Open and Relational Theology and Religious Pluralism.*

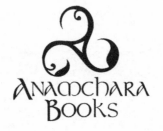

ANAMCHARA
BOOKS

AnamcharaBooks.com

Made in United States
North Haven, CT
08 December 2023

45235929R00071